The Adventures of Munford

Munford Meets Robert Fulton

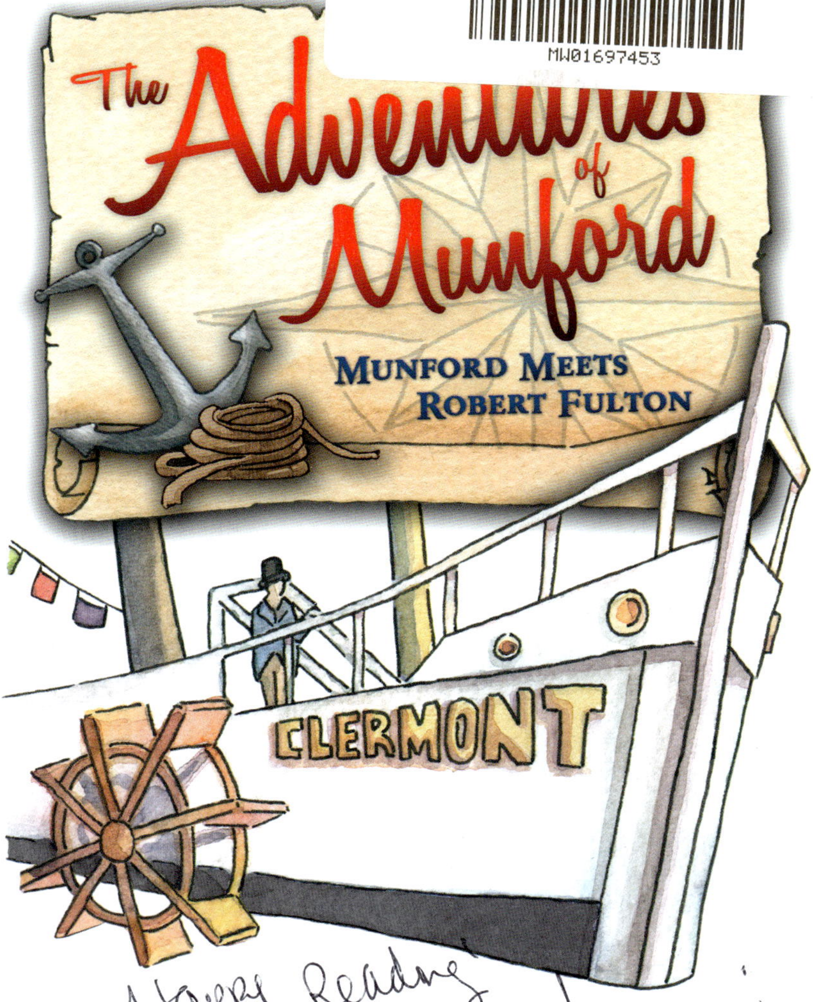

Happy Reading!
Jamie Aramini
Sept 2021

by Jamie Aramini

ILLUSTRATED BY
EMILY LEFFERTS

The Adventures of Munford

MUNFORD MEETS ROBERT FULTON

Written by Jamie Aramini
Illustrated by Emily Lefferts
Munford character and concepts created by George Wiggers

First Edition

Library of Congress Control Number: 2011924039
ISBN: 978-1-931397-70-4
Published in the U.S.A. by Geography Matters, Inc.®
800-426-4650
www.geomatters.com

Printed in the United States of America

Dedication

For Joey and James

Acknowledgements

Thanks to Josh and Cindy Wiggers for trusting me with your dream of Munford. I am honored to have the privilege to write this book.

Thanks to Emily Lefferts for bringing Munford alive with your beautiful illustrations.

Thanks to my parents for your unending dedication to me, my work, and helping me with the kiddos so I can write.

Thanks to Ian Z. for demystifying the inner workings of the steam engine for my very unmechanical brain.

Munford Meets
Robert Fulton
Oregon Country
Spanish Territory
Louisiana Purchase 1803
British Territory
Lake Superior
Lake Michigan
Lake Huron
Lake Erie
Lake Ontario
Albany
New York City
Lancaster
Philadelphia
New Orleans
Gulf of Mexico
Atlantic Ocean

Table of Contents

I couldn't believe I was here. This wasn't a part of the plan. It was July 4th, 1778. Two years ago today some brave men signed the Declaration of Independence. This important document said that the colonies in North America would be free from the rule of Great Britain. The colonists were still fighting for their freedom. Even so, people all over would be celebrating the anniversary of this important day. I had hoped to join in the festivities, but it wasn't looking promising.

My adventure began at a powder mill a few weeks ago. This is a place where the colonists made black powder. Black powder is another name for gunpowder and is mainly used to fire bullets from guns. I had arrived in a barrel of water.

I had hoped to escape, and I did manage to do that... as the barrel was dumped into the mill to make the black powder! As the gears turned, I became a part of the powder. I wasn't sure what it was going to be used for, perhaps in the guns that were fighting the American Revolution.

Powder seems very dry, doesn't it? It is hard to imagine that there might be any water in it, but there is. In fact, nearly everything around you has small amounts of water molecules.

Boy, was I mad! How would I celebrate Independence Day now? The black powder and I were dumped into another wooden barrel. Then it was sealed up tight. It looked like there was no hope of escaping now.

It was hard to tell what was going on from the inside. I think the powder was loaded up on a carriage. Then I was in a general store in Lancaster, Pennsylvania. (I knew because I could hear people talking—I couldn't see a thing from inside the barrel!) It was the third of July. Even if I made it out today, it looked like I wouldn't get to celebrate the Fourth. I overheard the storeowner talking with some customers, and the city of Lancaster had made some new rules this year. There was a shortage of candles because of the war. No one was supposed to light theirs, so all the fun would stop at dark. What kind of Fourth of July would that be?

I'm sorry, what was that? You want to know how I could fit inside a barrel? Haven't we met before? Silly me, always forgetting to introduce myself! My name is Munford. I'm just your average, everyday water molecule—one part oxygen, two parts hydrogen. Well... I guess I'm not exactly average. I'm an adventurer who travels the world in search of excitement. That's how I ended up at the signing of the Declaration of Independence. It's also how I ended up here in Lancaster, although I certainly hadn't seen any excitement yet.

Now that we've met, we better get back to the story. I heard the jingle of the door bell, then the voice of a young man. "Good morning, Mr. Fischer," said the boy.

"Hello, young Master Fulton. What mischief are you up to today?"

"Just buying some black powder," he said.

"What on earth for?" asked Mr. Fischer. He must have opened the barrel, because the next thing you know I was being scooped out and put into a powder horn. Luckily, I ended up as a smudge of powder on the outside so I could still see what was going on around me.

Now I could see the boy. He looked to be about eleven or twelve. He had dark hair and eyes and a mischievous grin. "The officials say I can't light a candle to celebrate the Fourth of July, so I am going to do something even better! I'm going to light up the night with a sky rocket!"

Mr. Fischer looked perplexed. “Light up the night sky? That’s impossible!”

Fulton paid for the powder and headed towards the door. “No sir, there is nothing impossible.”

Why did I suddenly feel like I was in for an adventure? This young boy definitely sounded like my kind of fellow. I couldn’t wait to see what he was up to.

The sky rocket would have to wait, as the boy headed straight to the school house. It was a small wooden building with lots of windows. Inside were desks filled with school children of all ages. A male teacher stood at the front, already started on the day’s lessons.

Robert must have been very excited about his school work. As the teacher talked, he kept wiggling around in his seat. He also drew on a piece of paper as he listened.

“Fulton! Answer the question!” The tall school teacher raised his voice from the front of the classroom.

Robert startled at the sound of his name. I could tell by the look on his face that he didn’t know what the question was. The teacher approached Robert’s desk.

He gave a sharp swat across Robert's hand with a ruler. "You must pay attention to your lessons!"

Robert frowned. "But, sir, you don't understand! My head is so full of ideas that I have no room left for your dusty books!"

The teacher was very angry now. "Out! Out! Out!" he shouted. Young Robert grabbed up his things and headed out the door.

He walked, in bare feet, down the city street. I had a great view from the powder horn that was hanging around his waist. He came to a large building with a sign above the door that read Isch & Messersmith. An illustration of a gun was below the name.

"Well, looky here, it seems we have a visitor," said a burly man standing beside the hot furnace.

"Quicksilver Bob!" said a younger, scrawny man who was mixing something up in the corner. "How did your school lessons go today?"

"The same as always," said Robert. "Gained nothing but bloody knuckles." He held up his hands as proof.

He pulled the piece of paper he had been drawing on from his bag. "Oh, but I did draw this up

while the schoolmaster thought I was practicing my spelling. I thought you might want to see it, Mr. Isch."

The burly man, who must have been Isch, came and got the paper from Robert. He took it over to his skinny friend, and they looked at it together. The men exchanged excited glances.

"Your eye for drawing is amazing, Robert," said Isch. "This looks like a working gun."

Robert jumped up from his seat and came over to the men. He flipped the paper over. "Yes, it is. I wrote the exact dimensions on the back—and the proportions for the powder."

Isch looked over the measurements carefully. "That schoolmaster must be a bumbling idiot! You are the most clever boy in all of Lancaster, and all he can see fit to do is rap your knuckles! Ridiculous, I tell you."

Robert shrugged. "I don't know about that. He says I will never amount to anything because I hate to read. He is probably right. I do hate reading!"

"Don't listen to that nonsense. Why don't you leave this sketch with me? Messersmith and I will look it over and see if maybe we can make this into a real gun."

"Really?" asked Robert eagerly.

"Really! This looks better than the sketches brought to us by grown men. And I'm positive that your math is exact." He leaned down and spoke quietly to Robert. "If we make this gun for you, will you tell us your secret?"

"My secret?" he asked.

"You know what I'm talking about. The mercury, or quicksilver as we often call it. Tell us why you are always buying quicksilver."

"I told you, Mr. Isch. It is for my experiments."

"What experiments? We want to know what

you have figured out. It must be spectacular since you refuse to tell anyone."

"I'm sorry, sir, but I'm afraid I must keep that to myself."

Isch sighed. "Okay, then. I guess all young boys are entitled to their secrets. We will just have to keep calling you 'Quicksilver Bob' until you decide to tell us. You are a lot like that quicksilver yourself, moving so fast none of the rest of us can keep up with you! We will still make the gun, though. Come by later in the week, and we will test it out."

Robert agreed. He gathered up his things and headed out the door. I liked him because he was always on the move to a new adventure.

Chapter Two

MR. HENRY'S BOAT

Robert kicked a rock with his foot as he walked. He must have known his mother would not be pleased with the trouble he had gotten into at school. He was not in any hurry to go home. After a little while, he turned down a dirt road. Where was he headed next?

We arrived at a large barn. There were chickens pecking about in front, and a large black and white cow chewing grass nearby. I noticed some of the wooden boards had come loose from the side of the barn. It looked like the place needed some work.

The inside of the barn was not full of animals as I thought it might be. Instead, it looked like some sort of laboratory, perhaps that of a mad scientist. There were nuts and bolts and levers and wheels, as

well as an assortment of machines and contraptions. In the corner, a pudgy older gentleman was tinkering with one of the machines. Robert watched quietly before clearing his throat.

"Oh, my!" said the man as he adjusted his glasses and smoothed his white hair with his hand. "Robert, my lad! Shouldn't you be in school?"

"The teacher kicked me out," he said.

The man plopped down onto a dirty work bench. "Why, whatever for?"

Robert stared at the ground. "He was angry because I told him there was no room in my head for his silly books!"

Robert looked up as he heard a chuckle. The chuckle became louder and louder until a tear ran down the man's cheek. Robert began to laugh, too, and soon they were both laughing as hard as they could.

"Come here, Robert."

The boy sat down on the bench. He didn't mind when the man put a greasy hand on his shoulder. "Your father would be so proud of you. You are a smart boy. You don't have too much school left. Just do your best to pay attention and learn what you can. Surely you could make some room for a few lessons in that big brain of yours!"

"I suppose I could, Mr. Henry."

"At least for your mother's sake, and the memory of your father..." There was a moment of silence before Mr. Henry spoke again. "But, enough of that! I found something today that I thought you might like! Let's go inside and have a look."

Robert followed Mr. Henry to the old farm house. Inside, he stood quietly in the front room while the old man went to get something from the back. As he stood, Robert looked at the beautiful pictures on the wall.

"Admiring the paintings?" asked Mr. Henry.

"Yes," said Robert. "They are magnificent."

Robert continued to stare at the paintings, mesmerized. "I think I would like to try that one day."

"I'm sure you would do an excellent job. I may have some old paints around here somewhere, perhaps a canvas or two. I'll get them out for you if I can find them in my messy barn."

"That would be wonderful!" said Robert, who now turned his attention to Mr. Henry.

The man was holding what looked like a large toy boat. “Remember that boat I was telling you about? The one that was powered by water?” Robert nodded. “This is the model I made after the boat was destroyed in the accident.”

Robert picked up the boat and looked it over. He could see the engine towards the rear, and the vessel had no sails like Robert was accustomed to seeing. “Why didn’t you rebuild it after the accident?” he asked.

“Too expensive. No one was interested anyway. But perhaps one day they will be.”

"Maybe I will make a boat of my own one day," said Robert. "I have already improved my fishing boat with a fantastic set of paddle wheels."

"Have you?" asked Mr. Henry. "What a smart idea!"

"I want to be like you," said Robert. "always trying to make new ideas work."

Mr. Henry smiled. "Well, I've had a good many more fail than succeed. You could do a lot better in life than trying to emulate old William Henry here. Maybe you should just stick to your art."

"Perhaps I can be an artist and an inventor," said Robert.

"Perhaps you can," said Mr. Henry. "Perhaps you can."

A while later, we left the Henry house. Robert had a small blank canvas and a collection of paints stashed in his school bag. He had yet to do anything with the powder in his powder horn, and I wondered if he had forgotten it altogether.

It was after dark when we finally arrived at the Fulton home. Robert quietly slipped into his bed. As he slowly drifted off to sleep, I remembered that tomorrow was July 4th. I wondered what Robert had planned.

Chapter Three

SKY ROCKETS

"Robert! Robert!" I awoke to the sound of a woman's voice calling. Didn't she know that my name wasn't Robert? My name is Munford, world famous explorer! Everyone knows who I am, don't they?

I heard a loud yawn, followed by the curtains being pulled back. Sunlight streamed into the room. Now I remembered where I was! I had spent the night at the home of young Robert Fulton. The boy quickly put on his clothes. He put on his powder horn, too, and I was glad he had not forgotten me. "Robert!" I heard again. I bet that was his mother calling.

He rushed down to the breakfast table, sat down, and filled his plate with eggs, biscuits, and a small slice of ham. There were several other children already at the table. These must have been his brothers and sisters. “Good morning, mother,” Robert said.

His mother didn’t smile. “Where were you, yesterday, Robert? Your teacher said that you were ill-behaved in class, and then he sent you out! You should have come straight home, young man.”

“I went to see William Henry. He is going to help me learn to paint. And he showed me this model of a boat...”

“I don’t care about your paintings or Mr. Henry’s boats, Robert. I care about your education. Since your father died, you are the man of this house. How will you ever make anything of yourself if you don’t complete your lessons?”

Robert got up and hugged his mother. “Oh, mother... I promise I will do something with myself. And when I do, I will buy you another farm just like the one Father bought you before he became ill.”

Robert’s mother seemed unimpressed. “I’ll believe it when I see it. In the meantime, you had better start working harder at school. I don’t want to see that schoolmaster’s face around here again, unless it is to tell me how well you are doing!”

"All right, Mother," Robert said. "But there's no school today, since it's the Fourth of July. I think I'll go to town and see if the gunsmiths are open."

His mother didn't argue, so we headed to town. Most of the shops were closed down, but Robert did not return home. He passed the day playing with some other children around town.

Later that evening, as we were returning home, I heard someone yelling. "Robert!" shouted a boy who met us on the street.

"Hello, Cyrus," said Robert. He waved at the boy, who was a bit shorter than him and had blond hair and bright blue eyes. "What are you doing today?"

"Oh, my mother has me out checking around to see if anyone will give us any bits of wax. We are nearly out of candles and cannot afford to buy any more with the prices the way they are."

Robert nodded. "The war will be over soon enough. Then we will be our own country, and there will be candles to go around for everyone!"

Cyrus rolled his eyes. "Now you're talking nonsense, Fulton. My papa says the war is going to last forever, and if it does end, it will be a King's victory."

"That means all the fighting would be in vain, Cyrus. All the deaths, even your own good brother, may he rest in peace." Cyrus lowered his head for a moment, but Robert kept on talking. "I hate this awful war, but let's hope it isn't all for nothing. When all is over, let's pray we shall be free!"

Cyrus let out a shout. "Hooray for freedom!"

Robert echoed him. "Hooray for freedom!" Both boys jumped, and the powder horn came loose and tumbled to the ground.

"What's that you've got there, Robert?"

"Oh, just some powder for my sky rockets."

"Your what?" asked Cyrus.

"Come and see!"

The boys raced back to Robert's house. I felt like I was holding on for dear life. They didn't take the smooth road, either. Nope! They insisted on running down the back paths, jumping through streams and climbing over fences. This wasn't the smooth cloud-sailing I was used to, that's for sure.

By the time we arrived at Robert's, I felt as sick as a dog. All that running had made me quite dizzy. I hoped we would be going to sleep soon, as the sun was just starting to set.

Robert opened up the powder horn. "You are going to love this, Cyrus," he said to his friend.

He began pouring the black powder into a long tube. I was trying to hold on to the powder horn as best as I could. I had just gotten out of the powder barrel. I certainly didn't want to end up in some tube!

From the corner of my eye, I saw Cyrus backing away. "Is... is... that d-d-dangerous?" he stuttered out.

"Yep!" answered Robert enthusiastically. Dangerous! Why, that was practically my middle name! I had been on many dangerous adventures and hadn't backed down yet. I was still hanging on when Robert gave the horn a good shake. Whoa! What was he doing? Trying to knock me off?

"There's just a little powder left on here and then we're good to go..." he said as he used his thumb to wipe the powder—and me!—right into the tube.

Everything was dark now. For a brief moment, I almost felt afraid. I kept thinking of how Robert had said this was dangerous. I tried to remember how danger didn't bother me. It didn't. Really.

There were a few moments of silence, and I felt the container being moved around. I heard some laughing and what sounded like the striking of flint. Wait a minute! Flint? That couldn't be a good sign.

Was it getting warm in here or was it just me? Whew! Things were really heating up, and fast. What was that sizzling noise?

All of a sudden I could see flames, and then I heard a loud bang! The next thing you know I was out of the tube and headed into the sky. I felt like I was being launched at full speed towards the stars. If I thought I was dizzy before, that was nothing. I found myself in the night sky, amid a flurry of bright lights.

It was a beautiful sight! I couldn't believe it! Robert was right—he had lit up the night sky with his rockets. I couldn't see his face from where I was, but I bet he was smiling. I felt like I had just taken the wildest ride of my life!

I wouldn't soon forget my adventures with the young Robert Fulton. He was a smart boy who seemed to have no fear of failure. I wondered what he was up to, but after he launched me into the sky, it looked there was no hope of returning to Lancaster.

There was plenty to do, however. America was still fighting for its freedom and I didn't want to miss out on anything. It would be quite a few years before the name Robert Fulton would enter my mind again.

Chapter Four

A FAMOUS BEN

The year was 1783. I had been wandering around the colonies for a while now, and a lot had happened in the last few years. The colonists had won the American Revolution. They were now free from the rule of Great Britain.

As for me, I was in a cloud again. It started out so peaceful and relaxing. I had plenty of time to daydream about my next adventure. I was thinking perhaps it was time to leave America in search of greener pastures—or better adventures, as the case may be.

It was about this time that I noticed that things were starting to get uncomfortable. I had less and less space to move around. The close quarters also left me with less quiet time for daydreaming. Pretty soon things started to get even worse. All of us water molecules were crammed so tightly together we could hardly move. Everyone was starting to get grumpy, too.

Just when things started to get really loud, I heard a cracking noise. Ouch... that sure was loud! I pushed and shoved my way down to the bottom to see if I could get a better view of what was going on outside of the cloud.

I looked out just in time to see a bolt of lightning hit the ground. It was followed by that loud cracking noise again. Thunder! I knew it. This wasn't just your average cloud; this was a storm cloud!

I sure was glad I paid attention to everything my Grandpa Gilbert had taught me about clouds. "This is something every water molecule needs to know," he had told me long before I had all these fun adventures under my belt. He taught me about stratus clouds (which almost always mean rain or snow) and cirrus clouds, which are way, way up in the sky. That type is great for casual travel, but kind of boring for an adventurer like myself! Lastly, he taught me about cumulus clouds, which look like big white balls of cotton in the sky.

I like cumulus clouds because they seem so friendly and happy. Usually all the other water molecules inside a cumulus cloud are pretty fun to hang out with. We have a good time just traveling around and stuff.

The problem with a cumulus cloud is that everyone wants to be in on the party. You can't blame us water molecules really, because we love a good time as much as anyone else. The more and more water molecules that show up, however, the bigger the cloud gets. The more crowded it becomes. Things start to get crazy, and then we aren't just a cumulus cloud anymore.

The cloud becomes a cumulonimbus. That's a big name for a big cloud! Cumulonimbus clouds get really big and really dark. The next thing you know, you'll be hearing the crack of thunder or seeing a flash of lighting. A storm has arrived, courtesy of yours truly, Munford, and all of my water pals!

Grandpa Gilbert taught me to stay away from cumulonimbus clouds. "Nothing but trouble, Munford, and not the good kind, either." Grandpa Gilbert said sometimes you had to face danger to have an adventure. That was the good kind of danger—the kind where you have to take a risk to achieve something good. The kind of danger in a storm cloud was still risky, but usually without any chance of good coming out of it (for the water molecules inside, at least).

I knew I couldn't hang on much longer. Woooooaaaaaaahhhhh! Another flash of lighting and now I was falling through the air, headed for the earth. The thunder sounded, and I saw that I was going straight for someone's house.

As I was plummeting towards what possibly could have been my demise, I noticed something quite peculiar. This house had a long pole sticking out from the roof. It looked like it might be metal, but it was hard to tell because I was moving so fast.

Flash! More lightning! This time, the lightning hit the pole attached to the house. What kind of crazy contraption was that? A device to catch lightning? I had never heard of such a thing.

I hit the roof of the house and tumbled right off the side, landing on a gentleman's shoulder with a splash. The man adjusted his glasses and looked up at the sky. What was he doing? Shouldn't he be inside instead of out here in all this weather?

"You really have done it, Franklin, my friend!"

I looked to see another man standing on the porch, looking out at the inclement weather.

"I told you, didn't I? You just had to see it for yourself!" said the man who must have been Franklin. "I've stopped the lightning from hitting the house. It strikes the rod and goes right into the ground instead of burning my house to the ground. Most of the houses in Philadelphia have lightning rods now, and they have kept many a fire from even starting. An ounce of prevention is worth a pound of cure, I say."

The rain continued to fall as Mr. Franklin hurried back into the house with his friend. I kept thinking and thinking. The name Franklin sounded so familiar to me. Who had I just met, and why did I have the feeling he was important?

I had the good fortune of spending the next few weeks with this Mr. Franklin character. Remember the one with the lightning rod? He was quite the interesting fellow. There were always people coming and going from his house, and I had learned quite a bit about him.

As luck would have it, I ended up with the best seat in the house for my time with Mr. Franklin. Well... maybe not the best seat, but certainly the one with the best view. After my fall from the rain cloud, I had ended up quite innocently on the old gentleman's hand. Maybe it was from standing out in all that inclement weather, but it soon appeared that Mr. Franklin had contracted a bit of a snuffly nose.

As the week progressed, Mr. Franklin diligently wiped his nose with an old, tattered handkerchief.

I had a bad feeling about what might happen next. These kinds of things always seem to happen to me.

Yep, you guessed it! In a moment of forgetfulness, Mr. Franklin didn't reach for his handkerchief. Instead, he wiped his nose with his bare hand, depositing me right inside his nose.

Now, I like Benjamin Franklin as much as the next person—maybe even more. No matter how much I liked him, however, I didn't like being on his nose hairs—not in the least bit. The whole place was warm and sticky. I tried and tried to pull myself loose, but to no avail. It looked like I was stuck here for the time being. At least I had a bird's eye view (or would

that be a bird's nose view?) of all the action!

Benjamin Franklin was a very busy man. For many years he had published *Poor Richard's Almanac.* He filled it with many words of wisdom, and I often heard people quote them when they came to visit him. "A penny saved is a penny earned," they would say. "Little strokes fell great oaks," was another phrase often repeated.

He had also helped write the Declaration of Independence with my old pal Thomas Jefferson. I knew I had met Ben somewhere before, and that must have been where it was.

Besides serving at the Constitutional Convention and as a diplomat to France, he was also an inventor. He created all kinds of things, including a wood stove. His Franklin stove was different from other wood stoves of the day, because it did a much better job at keeping a home warm. Mr. Franklin could have made a lot of money on his fancy stove, but he didn't even take out a patent for it. He wanted it to be available to as many people as possible to help them stay warm, even if he didn't get rich from it.

I really did like Benjamin Franklin. He was

such a smart man, always reading or writing or debating with someone. Oh, how he loved to debate. Just today, he was arguing about having his picture painted.

"Such a waste of time!" said Mr. Franklin. "I don't understand why I need yet another portrait painted of myself!"

His young assistant smiled. "Sir, you are a great man, and in a hundred years everyone will want to know what you looked like!"

"My appearance has very little to do with anything. Let them read all that I have written if they want to know what I looked like!"

Mr. Franklin eventually gave in. He thought it was silly to waste so much precious time posing for a picture. He was 76 years old now, and he seemed to be aware that his time on earth was growing short.

I went with him (still riding inside his nose, of course) to the studio where he was to sit for his portrait. A tall young gentleman was going to paint Ben's picture and took his time arranging Ben just the way he wanted him in a fancy chair. The artist didn't seem to mind me being there. Why, of course!

He was going to paint me into the picture as well. Who could blame him? Wouldn't I make an excellent addition?

Can't you see it? Dear old Ben sitting quietly with his gray hair and spectacles, probably thinking over something important like world peace or ending poverty. Then, me, Munford, perched inside his nose, just as stately. Of course, Mr. Franklin would have to hold his head up a little high for everyone to get a clear view of me. I straightened up and put on my best serious face. (One should never look too happy when being painted into a portrait with a great statesman, of course!)

Ben and the artist chatted while he worked. There was something about this boy that seemed so familiar, but I just couldn't seem to put my finger on it. He had dark hair and dark eyes. He spoke quickly, as he seemed to have a lot to say.

"What was your name again?" asked Ben, obviously impressed with this young painter.

"Robert Fulton, sir," said the boy.

Of course! It was all coming back to me now. Quicksilver Bob! This was the boy who had put me in the rocket and blasted me into the sky. I guess his wish had come true, and now he was painting pictures just like the ones that had been on the walls in Mr. Henry's home.

I listened as Robert told his story to Franklin. He was now 18. A few years ago, he felt that he had seen all that Lancaster had to offer. The small city was growing, but Robert wanted more. He wanted to learn more about painting and also provide a living for his mother and sisters. He was the man of the house, after all.

Mr. Isch, from the gun shop. had arranged for an apprenticeship for Robert in Philadelphia with a silversmith. As an apprentice, Robert would work for a set amount of time while learning the trade of silver work. He would then be able to work on his own.

It turned out Robert didn't like working for someone else very much. "So I decided to strike out on my own," he told Ben. "That was when I started painting portraits. I've made a pretty good living at it. In fact, I just saved up enough money to buy a farm for my mother and sisters."

Mr. Franklin was impressed. "What are you going to do next?"

The young man looked puzzled. "I guess I haven't really thought about it. I don't want to stay in Philadelphia forever, but I just don't know where to go from here."

Mr. Franklin had a lot of good ideas for Robert. "You simply must go to Europe. You can learn more about your craft. And make a decent living as well! Those silly Americans will pay you twice as much to paint their portrait in Paris as they will here. And don't forget the wonderful sights you could see..."

Robert seemed quite interested in the idea of going to Europe. I thought it seemed like a good idea, too... a new adventure! Before I had a chance to join him, though, Ben's portrait session was over for the day. I hoped I hadn't missed my chance.

It was a sunny day when Mr. Franklin returned to Robert Fulton's studio to take a look at the finished portrait. Imagine my surprise—no, my shock—when I saw the small portrait of the famous man. Let's just say it wasn't what I had expected.

I can't deny that young Fulton had done a good job. The portrait was quite life-like. It captured the aging gentleman's presence very well. There was just one tiny thing missing from the picture... me! That's right. In Robert's haste to finish the portrait, he had left out one of the most important details, Munford the water molecule.

I strained and strained my eyes, thinking perhaps I had just missed it. I could see Mr. Franklin's gray hair. His round eyes were just below that. Then...

his nose, with not even a trace of me! I tried not to act too disappointed. I'm sure his mistake was purely accidental. It didn't hurt my feelings too badly.

Mr. Franklin seemed quite pleased with Fulton's work. As he admired it, I looked around the studio. Many things that had been there before were now gone. Instead, there were several large trunks around the room.

Mr. Fulton pulled some things off of a shelf. As he did, a cloud of dust was stirred up. I watched as the dust filtered around the room, right towards Mr. Franklin and me. Ahhhhhchooo! Ben Franklin sneezed quite loudly. As he did, I flew from his nose

and landed with a splat on the chain of Robert Fulton's pocket watch. The young gentleman wiped his face and said, "God bless you."

"Thank you, Robert," said Ben. "I see you are packing up your things."

"Yes, I am. I am going to take your advice and go to Europe."

"How splendid," said Ben. "I know you will do very well, and I will be happy to write you a letter of reference. There will be so many good people excited to employ your talents while you are abroad."

I was glad to hear that Robert was going to Europe, especially now that I was with him. I could hardly wait to see what new journey awaited us.

The next few weeks were spent in anticipation. Robert had many preparations to make before we could depart. He sold his tiny studio and packed up all his things. He visited his mother and sisters and told them goodbye. I found myself much more at ease on his pocket watch than I had been in Mr. Franklin's nose.

It was a dreary day when we arrived at the docks for our departure. Our ship was quite enormous, with huge white sails that flapped in the wind. There were many people also boarding. Perhaps all of them were setting out on their own adventures.

The living conditions on board the ship were very cramped, and there was not a lot of room to move about. It reminded me a little bit of being in a storm cloud. Also like a cloud, we were entirely at the mercy of the wind. Sometimes it would blow at a decent pace, pushing our sails along. Other times, it would barely move at all, leaving us stalled in the water.

Our first week aboard, Robert became quite ill. I think the boat's rocking motion made him seasick. His face turned a little bit green, and he couldn't keep down any of his food. (Although, the food served on the ship didn't look very tasty anyway.)

Once he recovered from his illness, Robert wanted to explore every inch of the ship. I guess his fascination with boats had carried over from childhood. He looked over the sails, asking the crew all kinds of questions about them. He even went down to the galley and talked to the cook about what it was like cooking on the sea.

Robert was curious about everything. Sometimes he brought out his sketch book and drew pictures of the boat or the passengers. Several people even paid him for his drawings. As he sketched, he would talk to the other passengers. "If I ever have a ship," he would say, "it won't be as dirty as this one. I'll be sure my crew keeps it as clean as possible."

The other folks found his strange ideas funny. They all just accepted things the way they were, including the dirty ship. "Maybe you could make a faster ship, too, while you are at it," they would say with a laugh.

Robert didn't seem to notice their mocking voices. "Well, of course. When I build a boat, it will have an engine to propel it. It won't even need sails if I have my way."

This brought even more laughter. "No sails? An engine! Impossible!"

"There's nothing impossible," Robert would answer. "I've seen a boat powered by an engine with my own two eyes."

"On what ocean or river?" asked a passenger in reply.

"Well…" said Robert. "It was just a model, but my friend William Henry built the boat and tested it on the water. It was destroyed in an accident, but it did work."

"What fanciful ideas you have in that head of yours!" said one man.

"Fanciful is such a kind word," said another. "I think his head is full of lies."

"Think what you want," answered Robert. "But if I ever build a boat, you will see that I am right."

The men just chuckled. "You are a good artist. You should do what you are good at and put this boat engine nonsense out of your head."

I wasn't sure what to believe. I, too, had seen Mr. Henry's boat model, but I had never seen it actually in use on the water. Perhaps it hadn't wrecked, but had never worked at all. If Mr. Henry had even built it in the first place, that is.

If anyone could make a faster boat, they would be very rich and famous. An engine would do the trick, but how would it be powered? Could an engine powerful enough to propel a small boat be built? Much less a big ship? There were so many questions to think of.

I was glad that Robert was not hurt by what those unkind men had said. I wouldn't like it one bit if someone said I had a head full of lies! Would you? I remembered Robert's sky rockets, which he had been told would never work. He had been right about those, hadn't he? Maybe there was nothing impossible!

It looked like I would never find out. A few weeks into our voyage, we crossed paths with a terrible storm. (What did I tell you about those cumulonimbus clouds? Nothing but trouble!) The ship's captain told everyone to get below deck, but Robert didn't listen. He wanted to see the storm for himself. All the deck hands were so busy with the boat, I don't think they had time to notice him.

He watched as lightning flashed in the sky, and soon huge pieces of hail began to pelt the boat. Still, Robert did not go below deck. The wind blew so fiercely that it ripped a hole in one of the sails. Finally, someone noticed Robert and told him to get below deck before he was killed. He nodded and headed that direction, but a huge wave rocked the boat and he lost his balance. As the wave's water washed over

the boat's deck, Robert was drenched. The wave knocked me loose from his pocket watch and into the ocean. I couldn't help but feel sad at my separation from Mr. Fulton.

The next few years passed by in a hurry. I kept looking for adventure, as I always do. I also kept my ears open for any mention of Robert Fulton. I thought I heard his name mentioned while I was in London, England. Something about a display of his paintings at an art gallery, I think. I didn't get to check it out, however, before a cold front swept through and took me with it.

We need to move forward a few years to pick up the next important parts of our story. It was now a cool March morning in 1803. The fog rolled off of the River Seine into the city of Paris, France, early in the morning. It was a fine gray mist, made up of millions of tiny water molecules. Right in the middle was your favorite—me!

Fog is much like being in a cloud, except we are so close to the ground that we can touch it! As we traveled through the city, I found myself at the market. The merchants had just begun stacking up their goods.

There were big, crusty loaves of bread piled high in woven baskets. There were colorful vegetables stacked in worn wooden crates. There were large blocks of cheeses in pale white, creamy yellow, and even a vivid orange color.

Customers slowly began arriving at the market. They stopped to buy large brown eggs, shiny silver fish, and bright red flowers. The sun had begun to warm up the chilly morning air, causing the fog to clear away, and leaving me as part of a tiny drop of dew on a green pear.

"Bon jour," the customers greeted the merchants.

"Au revoir," the merchants told them as they left the booths.

"Merci!" a young boy thanked his mother for buying him a small piece of candy.

There were so many words to learn: *pain* for bread, *ouef* for egg, *fromage* for cheese. The fish were called *poissons*, the flowers *fleurs*, and the candy *bonbons.*

The lively sounds of a fiddle soon filled the air, and I saw a young man playing in the center of the market. Folks gathered around him, tapping their feet with the music. When he finished his song, everyone clapped. Some people threw small coins in the open fiddle case at his feet.

I saw another young man as well, sitting on a small stool in front of a wooden easel. He held a small piece of lead in his hand and moved it quickly over the paper on his easel. From time to time, a pretty lady would stop and sit in the chair across from him. He would quickly sketch her portrait and then give it to her in exchange for a few coins or some food. It reminded me of my old friend Robert Fulton. I wondered what he was up to, and if he still made a living painting pictures of important people.

"*Poire*?" asked a woman as she approached the table where I was. The merchant pointed to the pears. She looked them over. I hoped she would pick the pear that I was on. I didn't want to get stuck here all day!

She picked up a pear and felt it with her fingers. "Too soft," she said as she returned it to the basket. She picked up another and felt it as well. "Too hard."

Pick me! Pick me! Pick me! I don't think she could hear my shouting as she seemed to pick up every pear but my own.

Finally, she reached her hand down and picked up my pear. She squeezed it, nearly crushing me in the process! "Just right," she said. She handed the man a few francs and then walked away with me and the pear in tow. I sure was glad this kind lady had bought my pear. Now I knew I wouldn't be stuck where I was. The key to finding adventure, I think, is to always be on the move. Adventure doesn't come to you—you have to come to the adventure!

She stopped for a moment in front of the fiddler. She hummed along with the lively tune he was playing, then placed my pear right in his fiddle case. Oh, dear! I hadn't even made it out of the market.

I sat patiently in the fiddle case waiting for something to happen. It seemed like hours and hours without excitement, except for the occasional hit by a stray coin being tossed inside. Finally, the young

gentleman gathered his earnings into a small sack and put his fiddle away.

He took a bite out of the juicy green pear, narrowly missing me in the process. I really hoped he wouldn't eat me. I've been on that journey many times, and I have to say it isn't very pleasant. All the painful chewing and sticky saliva, followed by a long slide down the esophagus. Then there's the stomach and the intestines (both large and small). It is warm and gooey and dark. Not a pleasant place for a water molecule, let me tell you!

He kept eating his pear, and I kept trying to avoid him. Finally, there was hardly anything left but the stem, which I was clinging to. He tossed the stem and all onto the street.

The nerve of some people! Just tossing me onto the street like a common piece of trash. Did he even stop to think about my well-being? I think not! Well, at least he didn't eat me. Where would I end up now?

There was no chance of survival on this busy street in Paris. A horse kicked me with his hoof. A little boy stomped on me with his shoes. (I'm pretty sure he did it on purpose.) The stem and I rolled down the street, pushed by a gust of wind. Just when I thought things couldn't get any worse, a pigeon landed beside me. She peered down at the pear stem. and looked at it for a minute before scooping it up in her beak.

She flew up into the air—and then the unthinkable happened. She swallowed the stem of the pear whole. I now found myself inside the pigeon's digestive tract. Just in case you are wondering, it wasn't any better than a human's. It was dark and damp and I think it smelled a little fishy.

I'm not sure how long I was inside the bird. All I know is that it was too long. Eventually I came out of the bird, along with a lot of other, well... waste. It was pretty gross, especially when the whole mess landed with a splat on someone's hat. Little did I know, it happened to be the hat of one of the most important men in France.

I looked out from my spot on this black hat, wondering how on earth I was ever going to get out of this gooey mess. I had hoped the owner of the hat would clean me off, but it seemed that my unfortunate arrival had gone unnoticed. He was too interested in the conversation at hand.

The group of gentleman sat around an ornate iron table in a lovely garden. I spotted beautiful yellow roses and lush green shrubs. A stone path led to a huge building, which I could only assume to be some sort of palace. They all talked in quiet voices.

They were discussing the unfortunate predicament that the country of France was currently in. They were in a war with Great Britain and the entire British navy had blockaded the French coast.

"We must demonstrate that we have the stronger navy. A victory against Britain would make it plain to everyone that France is the leading power of the world." These words were spoken by the owner of my hat.

"Napoleon, sir, with all due respect, Britain's navy is larger and stronger than our own. To defeat them is nearly impo—"

"Don't even say it!" said Napoleon in reply. I recognized the name Napoleon—I must have been on the hat of Napoleon Bonaparte! I had heard his name several times while I was on the streets of Paris. He had forcefully taken the throne of France and now wanted to take over other countries as well. He was really at odds with Great Britain, who thought he was getting too powerful.

Napoleon continued to talk. "I am not world famous for my military strategy for nothing," he said (without a trace of humility, might I add). "Surely we can outsmart them, even if their resources outnumber our own."

The men discussed various ideas of taking down the British navy. Each involved complicated military campaigns. It also meant taking valuable troops away from the other battles Napoleon was fighting.

"We need more funds," one man suggested. "Perhaps you should consider the offer from President Jefferson—"

Napoleon cut him off before he could finish. "Never. I will not sell New Orleans. The city is too important for my plans in the Gulf of Mexico."

"Sir, I understand wanting to keep the city, but what good is it to us? It is in an entirely different hemisphere. It is vulnerable to enemy attack because it is so far away. Not to mention, it would seem silly to lose the battle on the home front because we needed money we could have gotten from New Orleans."

Napoleon was silent for a moment. "I see your point, but let's not think of that now. Let us focus on the task at hand, which is destroying the British navy. Surely someone must have an idea?"

"Well, there is one other thing," said another member of the group. "There is an American living in Paris. He has been in and out of the palace for over a year trying to get us to look at his crazy scheme."

"Crazy scheme?" Napoleon seemed very interested.

"Yes. He has designed a diving boat. It is supposed to go underwater for several hours at a time. He says it can be outfitted with weapons to sink ships. The ships, of course, would never see anything coming because all would be underwater."

Napoleon slammed his fist to the table. "Why is this the first I have heard of him? This sounds like an excellent plan to defeat the British."

"Well, sir, the boat is not yet complete. He wanted money from the French government to help fund his experiments. Nearly everyone thinks he is a lunatic, sir. He just stopped by a few days ago to tell us the boat was almost ready and we could stop by to see him demonstrate it."

I could barely see Napoleon wringing his hands in excitement over the brim of the hat. "Well, what are we waiting for? I want to see this diving boat!"

It was several hours before the demonstration could be arranged. A messenger was sent to tell the boat maker to prepare for Napoleon's visit. Napoleon and his men ate a fancy lunch at their garden table, and then prepared to head to the River Seine to see what was going on with this curious boat.

I was excited to see not only the boat, but also who this man was that had created it. I had developed a certain fondness for the Americans during my time spent there. I wondered if this American was someone I would recognize, or a new person altogether. Either way, I was sure that the day would lead to, at the very least, a small adventure.

We arrived at the docks sometime in the middle of the afternoon. The weather was cooperating, with the bright sun shining overhead. The men pointed out the new boat, which appeared

to be made of some kind of metal. It didn't really look that different from any of the other boats that were docked there.

A man appeared from below deck. He was very tall with striking dark hair and eyes. Why, this wasn't just any American—this was my old friend Robert Fulton! I couldn't believe it. Our paths had crossed again after all this time.

Chapter Nine

The Nautilus

Robert Fulton wasted no time in getting the demonstration under way. He gave a quick shout, "Introducing the *Nautilus*, France's first diving boat!" Then he waved from his spot on the boat deck, and descended along with the other crew members out of sight. What were they doing down below? How would they see to navigate if no one was above deck to see?

Since we had left the confines of the palace, Napoleon had become quite a different man. He was quiet and calm and almost cold. He made no comments upon seeing the boat, but I got the feeling that he was unimpressed. He tapped his foot as the boat started to move forward.

Well, this was spectacular—a boat. I didn't understand what all the fuss was about. It looked just like any other boat on the dock that day, including the large white sails that flapped in the wind. It sailed for several feet, and I wondered if Napoleon was going to leave at any moment. But just as I was really starting to think old Quicksilver Bob had lost his marbles, a peculiar thing happened.

The boat's sails closed up. Where was he going to go without sails? It was bad enough that he was below deck where he could see nothing, but now he had no sails! What would he do now?

Wait! Now the boat was sinking! Fulton and his crew mates were going to drown! The crowd

seemed unaffected as the boat slipped further and further underwater.

"Help!" I shouted as loudly as I could but no one seemed to notice. "Help! That boat is sinking!" I yelled and yelled and yelled. Still nothing. Napoleon kept tapping his foot until the boat was completely out of sight.

Well, maybe before I had thought of Napoleon as an unfriendly man, but now I knew he was just downright mean. It wasn't just him, though. It was the entire group of spectators. None of them seemed to care that the boat was now lying at the bottom of the river.

I hung my head in sadness. I hadn't gotten to spend a lot of time with Mr. Fulton, but I had still come to think of him as a friend. Minutes passed in silence as the crowd watched the water, obviously saddened at the loss of this great inventor.

"Well," said someone in the crowd. "It isn't surprising. That man was a lunatic, thinking he could take a boat underwater like that and survive."

"Others have done it before," said someone else.

"But they didn't make it out alive! And neither has Fulton."

Napoleon stopped tapping his foot and turned to go. I took one last look back at the watery grave of Robert Fulton. It was such a tragedy, and not at all the kind of adventure I was hoping for today.

"Wait a minute! Look there!" shouted a little boy.

Everyone turned to the water. I saw nothing except the smooth, calm surface of the river. "Over there, don't you see those bubbles?"

Sure enough, hundreds of feet away, the water was bubbling like a boiling pot of water. What could it be? Surely not...

The crowd gasped and soon the air was filled with voices. What did those bubbles mean? Was it simply the last bit of air released from the sinking boat? Then why was it so far away from where the boat had started?

"I see it! There it is!" someone from the crowd shouted.

Bonaparte leaned forward. It was true. Slowly, out of the water came the *Nautilus*. "He's traveled nearly 400 feet," Napoleon whispered to the man beside him.

The whole crowd was clapping and cheering

now as the diving boat was fully above surface. Robert was the first to come out. He waved to the crowd and took a little bow.

Napoleon and his men quickly made their way to the boat. He inspected the *Nautilus* thoroughly, his nose high in the air as he looked it over. He acted like he didn't care about this silly boat at all. The men were introduced. I was right, this was Robert Fulton! I guess he had given up on his painting after all and taken to the high seas! I knew he would make a great inventor, and what I saw today had proved just that.

"It needs a lot of work," said Napoleon.

"Yes," said Robert. "There was some minor leaking while we were under water. I'm convinced it could be sealed up better in no time. If France would just be willing to invest some money in the project..."

"I'll give you 60,000 francs," said Napoleon.

Robert's eyes widened in shock. "60,000! That would be marvelous! With that amount of money, I could make all the improvements that are necessary—"

Napoleon kept talking with total disregard for anything Robert was saying. "I will pay you the full sum once you have destroyed a British warship. They have nearly surrounded the coast of my country, and if your silly boat can destroy one, then I will pay."

"You will pay after I destroy a ship?"

Napoleon nodded.

Robert frowned. "With all respect, without the funds ahead of time to make the improvements, I highly doubt I will be able to defeat even the smallest ship."

"Four hundred thousand francs if you can destroy a thirty gun warship, Fulton."

Robert gulped. Four hundred thousand francs! That was a lot of money! "Yes, sir," said Robert. "Yes, sir."

I felt a little bit sorry for Robert. I imagined he had worked very hard on his boat. I wondered how he had managed to pay for it all. Surely he had not painted that many portraits!

"I will be leaving the country soon for battle," said Napoleon. "But you can report back to one of my men on your progress. They will settle your account for you."

Robert nodded his head. At that same moment,

a gust of wind blew through. Napoleon's hat flew from his head and directly into the water. Fulton was the first to react. He reached over the edge of the ship's deck and rescued the hat from the water. He gave it a good shake, flinging me onto the lapel of his jacket as he did.

"I'm so sorry, sir," said Robert as he handed the leader of France his hat. Napoleon did not respond. He took his hat and walked curtly off of the *Nautilus*. Well, I had made it back to my friend Robert. Not to mention, I wasn't at all sad to see Napoleon go.

Chapter Ten
ROBERT LIVINGSTON

My time with Robert didn't start out too adventurous. In other words, he had not yet stuck me in a tube and sent me into the sky. For the longest time, Robert sat on the deck of the boat recording some calculations in his notebook. He seemed a little down, perhaps because Napoleon had not agreed to give him the money. He looked up when someone called out his name. "Robert Fulton?"

"Yes," he said.

A tall gentleman stepped on board. "My name is Robert Livingston. I work for the American government here in France."

Robert sighed. "If you've come to give me another message from Bonaparte, it isn't necessary. I'll do my best to accomplish what he asks, but..."

"No, no, no. I heard about your little display today with the diving boat. The *Nautilus* you call it?"

"Yes, it was just a demonstration. She still needs some work."

"That's what I'm here about. Word has it you are trying to sell the boat to Bonaparte?"

Robert frowned. "Not sell it so much as perhaps get an investment. I think with some work she could be a wonderful asset to the French navy. Everyone knows the British have a better, stronger navy, but with an improved *Nautilus* on the French side, everything would change."

Livingston nodded. "Have you considered selling your invention to the British?"

"I've spoken with several governments. They all want exclusive rights. I refuse to sell a weapon that could possibly be one day used against my own country. I'm an American, sir, and that is where my loyalties lie. I will never allow my inventions to go to waste if my country needs them!"

"I applaud your patriotism, kind sir. Perhaps you are in the wrong line of work however. A purveyor of weapons so powerful cannot have such loyalties hindering him."

"I lost many close to me in the American Revolution. I hate war and all the trappings that go along with it. My only hope is that I can design a weapon so powerful, so frightening, so deadly that it will create peace. No one will want to fight when the consequences are dire."

Livingston replied, "Do you not fear that someone will create a more powerful weapon?"

"It is a possibility, I suppose," said Fulton. "One I am willing to contemplate. For now, I will keep working on the *Nautilus* until I achieve my goal of peace or run out of funds, whichever comes first."

As the men were talking, I noticed that I was getting a little warm. Oh, no! I was getting really warm. I was going to evaporate, and then I would once again be separated from Robert Fulton. I had hoped to stick around long enough to see how things turned out with his diving boat.

"That is actually what I am here to see you about," said Livingston. "I have a proposal for you. I have heard a lot about you, and I would like to invest in your work. There are a lot of ideas in this old brain of mine, but no talent or skills to bring them about. I also have deep pockets, something which I am told you sorely lack."

Fulton chuckled. "I'm glad to see my state of poverty is well-known, but I won't have a boss. I will do what I want when I want. I may, however, be willing to accept you as a partner."

I turned into a vapor and went floating through the air. Oh, well, I guess no more diving boat for me. In fact, I was headed straight towards Mr. Livingston's face. I hoped I wouldn't end up in his nose.

"It would do you good," said Livingston. "I have a lot of contacts, both here in France and in America as well. I can provide you with the investors you need as well as the publicity to get your projects off of the ground."

Fulton seemed pleased with this explanation. The men shook hands, and a partnership was formed. Meanwhile, I landed on Mr. Livingston's eyelash. He blinked, and I ended up in his eye.

Have you ever been in someone's eye before? I have, a couple of times. It isn't as dark as a person's nose, except at night. Then it gets really dark! During the day it is pretty bright and cheerful. It is also pretty

clean. The eye does a great job of keeping yucky stuff out.

Floating around Mr. Livingston's eye was a nice change of pace. This was quite different from where I normally end up—on a hat or a coat or something. It was an interesting place to be. His irises were constantly adjusting the size of his pupils, depending on how bright it was. I also had a great view of everything that was going on. This turned out to be a good thing, as I would soon witness one of history's important moments!

Mr. Livingston departed the *Nautilus*. I felt hopeful that I would see Mr. Fulton again, since I was now residing in the eye of his business partner. Until then, I planned to find as much adventure as I could.

Chapter Eleven
An Important Purchase

At first, I wasn't sure if I would enjoy my time with Mr. Livingston. He seemed like a nice man, but would there be an adventure in store? I'm certainly not the kind of water molecule to just sit around and do nothing. I need to get in on the action!

One thing I noticed was that this Livingston fellow liked to talk. His office almost always had somebody in it. Lots of traveling Americans came to visit him. He also had many visits from members of the French government. He talked about all kinds of things, including Robert Fulton and his important work. I still wasn't exactly sure what Mr. Livingston's job was here in France, until I overheard him talking to his aide.

"I'm afraid there is no hope," Livingston told the younger man. "Napoleon will never part with

New Orleans, and President Jefferson will be sorely disappointed. The United States would benefit greatly from owning such a strategic city."

My ears perked up at the mention of President Jefferson. He and I go way back. Maybe you didn't know this, but I helped Jefferson write the Declaration of Independence. Okay... maybe I didn't help him write it exactly. But I was there. In fact, I got stuck in the ink of one of the signatures!

"Don't give up hope yet, sir," said the aide. "I do believe Napoleon will change his mind. He is prone to change it as often as the weather changes here in Paris."

"New Orleans is such a small part of the vast territory of Louisiana. The money—ten million dollars!—would be such a help in his war with Britain."

So that was why Livingston was here! My old friend Jefferson had sent him to purchase the city of New Orleans. Why did the French own New Orleans anyway? It was so far away from their country. It was much closer to the newly formed United States, wasn't it?

I wished that I could tell Livingston what I had heard when I was with Napoleon. I bet he would like to know that the French leader was actually thinking about selling New Orleans. If only I had landed in his ear rather than his eye! Then he might have been able to hear me.

A few days after my arrival, a messenger came to Mr. Livingston's office with very important news. Mr. Bonaparte agreed to see him and his delegates to discuss New Orleans that same day. Mr. Livingston seemed quite surprised, but of course I wasn't at all. Everyone rushed about preparing for this important meal. A horse-drawn carriage took the men to Napoleon's palace.

They were led into a large room with a very long table that ran down the middle. Each man took a seat and in a few minutes Napoleon arrived. I noticed he was still wearing his funny hat from the last time I had seen him.

Everyone exchanged pleasantries, respectfully addressing Napoleon as "First Consul." I thought that was a pretty fancy name, although it was a few months later when I learned he had changed his title to "Emperor."

The room became quiet as the Americans waited for Napoleon to make some sort of offer. He leisurely sipped his tea as he gazed out the window. Livingston took a drink of his own tea. He was probably wondering how long we would sit there in silence before Napoleon spoke what was on his mind.

"I will take twenty million," said Bonaparte.

Livingston's eyes went wide. I knew from my time with him that he only had access to ten million. The newly formed United States simply didn't have the resources to pay any more than that for the city of New Orleans.

"Sir, I am delighted to hear that you have decided to entertain our offer," said Livingston. "However, I'm afraid that the most I am prepared to offer for New Orleans is eight million."

Bonaparte set his tea cup down, still looking out the window. "New Orleans? Didn't you receive my message? I am not offering you the city, but the entire territory of Louisiana."

Livingston immediately choked on his tea, the warm brown liquid spilling down the front of his shirt.

A servant quickly handed him a napkin. He blotted at his shirt as he muttered the word, "Louisiana?"

"Are you hard of hearing? Yes, Louisiana. My aides tell me it will double the size of your country to make such a purchase. I am more than willing to offer my assistance in this, not to mention the added benefit that it will make Britain furious."

Livingston looked at the other men with him. This was not part of the plan, but how could he pass up such an offer? "Sir, my government has only authorized me to spend ten million dollars."

Napoleon sighed. "Fifteen million for all of Louisiana." He set his cup down and headed

towards the door. "And I'd like an answer in the morning."

I watched as Livingston and the other men talked over the offer in hushed tones. "We must act right away. You know how Bonaparte is. If we don't take his offer he could change his mind at any moment!"

"It will take weeks to confer with President Jefferson, to request the additional funds from Congress. What would we do with all that land anyway? Let us make a counter-offer for New Orleans only."

"It seems foolish to pass up an offer for so much land at such a low price," said Livingston.

"I think he is offering the land so cheaply because he knows it is worthless," someone said. "The Louisiana desert, some call it!"

"No," said Livingston. "I say we take it. Who knows what important untapped resources are in that vast range of unexplored land? Even if part of it is desert, it may have things our growing country can use."

So it was decided. The United States would now double in size. It would cost the developing country less than three cents per acre. I was pretty glad that I got to witness this historic purchase.

Later in the week, Mr. Livingston shared the exciting news with his friend and business partner, Robert Fulton. "It looks like my work here in Paris is done," he told him.

Mr. Livingston must have been really sad about the Louisiana Purchase, because as he shared the story a tear came to his eye. His eyelid filled up with salty liquid. As the tears brimmed over and down his cheek, I went with them. "How embarrassing!" said Mr. Livingston. "These are tears of joy over completing my task here in Paris!"

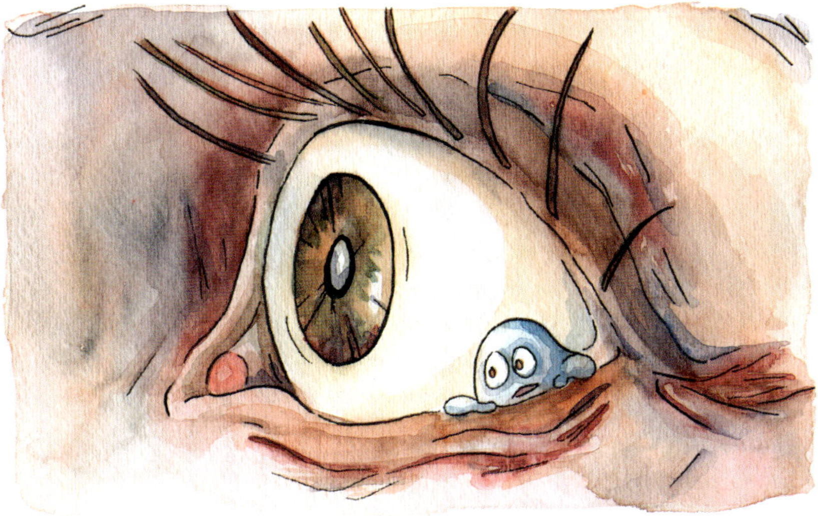

I guess he wasn't sad then, but happy. Mr. Fulton handed him a handkerchief, and he wiped the tears (and me) from his cheek before handing it back to his friend. Mr. Fulton tucked the handkerchief in his front pocket. The top stuck out just enough so that I could still see what was going on.

If Mr. Livingston was leaving Paris, it only made sense that his friend and business partner go with him. I listened intently as the men discussed their plans for the future. The *Nautilus* had never been able to destroy a British warship in battle.

There was one other project that the men had worked on. It was another boat, and they hoped to demonstrate a working version before departing Paris to return to New York. This would not be a diving boat, but a regular one that was powered by an engine. The engine would run on the power of steam. It would be similar to the model boat Fulton had seen at the home of his childhood neighbor, William Henry.

Livingston couldn't wait to see the completed

project. He had total confidence in Fulton's abilities. It seemed like he was the only one with such a positive outlook, because on more than one occasion I had heard the dock workers talking about Mr. Fulton's boat. "That man is stark raving mad! A boat powered by steam? Doesn't he know it has been tried a thousand times before? Nary a time has worked, either."

The other men laughed. "It will be like that diving boat of his. The *Nautilus*, was it? It may work for a while, but he will lose interest before he gets around to completing it."

"I wonder what he will name it?" someone asked.

"Perhaps he shall name it *Fulton's Folly*!"

Everyone must have thought that was terribly clever, because the whole group erupted into a fit of laughter. Grandpa Gilbert had once taught me what the word *folly* means, which is basically "silly mistake." It didn't seem like a very nice thing to name a boat, did it?

Everywhere I went with Mr. Fulton, I heard the same thing. Some folks would whisper "Fulton's

folly" under their breath, but others were not so timid. They came right out and told Mr. Fulton that his boat would never work.

Mr. Livingston continued to support Fulton with both money and positive morale as he was preparing to return to the States. He encouraged his powerful and wealthy friends to help pay for Fulton's work. As for me, I was getting a little bored with it all. I had been on the boat several times, but there was still no steam engine in sight.

Even those who supported Fulton weren't very proud of it. I am of the opinion that Livingston had kind of twisted their arms into helping him out. But they didn't want anyone to know what they were doing.

Just like today. A man came aboard the boat with some money for Robert, and handed over an envelope that was filled with cash. "Here is my investment for your steamboat project. Livingston has convinced me that this project will succeed. He thinks you are much closer to completion than what everyone is saying. Is it true?"

"Of course," said Fulton. "Would you like me to tell the papers of your involvement? That you are on board for the creation of this modern marvel?"

The man looked over his shoulder, as if he was checking to see if someone might be watching him. "Oh, no, no, that's fine, really. Not necessary at all. I'm a quiet man, after all. No need to draw attention to myself."

"You're ashamed?" asked Robert. "Embarrassed to be helping this crazy old fool?"

"Well, I wouldn't say that exactly. It's just that Livingston has assured me this is a sound investment, but just in case... I don't want to be mocked if things were to go... well, pardon the pun, under."

Mr. Fulton respected this gentleman's wishes, as well as others who wanted to keep their privacy. He didn't tell the public who was paying for his experiments with the engine. He continued to work around the clock to ready the boat for the big day, so that he could return to America. He worked so much that he didn't even take time to wash his dirty handkerchief.

I wondered if he even remembered that Mr. Livingston had soiled it with his tears. Did he even notice that I was there? Listening in on all his conversations? Following his every move as he worked?

Finally the day came when the engine was installed on the boat. The huge contraption looked a little too complicated to me. How would it all work? After the engine was ready, we retired to Mr. Fulton's small apartment for the night. I was so glad to finally have a break. All this boat building was harder work than you might expect. Especially for a small guy like me—all that heavy lifting and what not.

It was nearly impossible to rest because of the anticipation. Tomorrow was the big day! We would finally show the world the steamboat that we had worked so hard on. Everyone would know that Fulton was not a fool, but a great inventor and engineer. At least I hoped so. I had yet to see the engine work, so even I was a little unsure.

"Sir! Sir! Wake up!" My eyes slowly opened. What was all this noise? A lantern was lit, and there was Robert in his pajamas staring at one of his workers. I watched from my spot, where Mr. Fulton had casually tossed his coat over the back of a chair.

"What is it, son? Can't you see I'm sleeping?"

"Sir! It's the boat! She has sunk to the bottom of the river. I think the weight of the engine was too much, or perhaps someone slashed her hull. It's hard to say, except, well, she's gone!"

Robert was rushing around now, pulling on his clothes and boots, muttering some unkind words that I won't repeat here. He tossed on his jacket, and once again we were out in the cool night air.

The next twenty-four hours passed in a flurry. Robert's men dived to the bottom of the River Seine. They took the boat apart piece by piece and returned it to shore. Even Robert himself dived into the chilly water. Sadly, he forgot to remove his coat before he did. His handkerchief, with me barely hanging on, floated out into the River. It looked like I would never know the fate of the steamboat.

I watched from the water as the men kept pulling pieces of the boat up. When all was over, the whole glum group sat and stared at their work, sopping wet and split to pieces. It wasn't a pretty sight. Perhaps *Fulton's Folly* was a good name after all.

Chapter Thirteen
THE CLERMONT

The next few months passed by slowly. I got washed off of the handkerchief by the river water, and floated down the Seine River and into the English Channel. From there, I ended up in the Atlantic Ocean.

I spent a long time in the ocean. The ocean is a fun place. I got to see a lot of different wildlife—a humpback whale, a gray shark, and even a loggerhead turtle. It was very cool, if I do say so myself!

Eventually, I got swept up in a hurricane somewhere in the Gulf of Mexico. Then, I ended up back in the United States again! Can you believe it? I even ran into my old friend Thomas Jefferson, who was sending some important men to explore the

Louisiana Territory. Meriwether Lewis and William Clark were their names, and I ended up joining them on their epic journey. It was pretty wild, but I don't have time to tell you about it here.

After traveling all across the continent of North America with Lewis and Clark and their men, I ended up in the Pacific Ocean. Is it just me or do I spend a lot of time in oceans? Maybe it is because nearly three-fourths of the earth's surface is made up of oceans!

Finally, several trips through the water cycle later, I ended up in New York City. (Check your map, because it is on the other side of the continent from the Pacific Ocean!) As fate would have it, I arrived in town on a very important day.

I was just hanging out, minding my own business in the Hudson River. It was a little chilly, but I had plenty of time to check out what was going on at the dock. There were lots of spectators just milling around, and I wasn't exactly sure what they were there for. I could only catch bits and pieces of the various conversations. Eventually, I heard the name Robert Fulton. He was here, in New York City! He was going to show everyone his new boat, the *Clermont*.

It appeared that all of New York City had turned out for today's demonstration. It reminded me of the *Nautilus* and the day I thought that Mr. Fulton had died. Except here, even more people were watching than had been in Paris.

The dock workers, with their dirty clothes and distinct fishy smell, all seemed to be taking breaks from their work to watch the new boat. Then there were the businessmen, in their fancy clothes, trying their best not to get dirty. I think they had shown up just to watch Robert fail. There were plenty of ladies, too, dressed in frilly dresses with their matching parasols. It seems that this had become something of a social event.

Would the *Clermont* work? Or would it sink to the bottom of the river as his first attempt did? Perhaps something even crazier would happen, like the entire boat exploding in flames. The whole dock was in a frenzy of excitement!

The boat was quite a sight. It was much larger than the others on the river—150 feet long and weighing 160 tons (which is about 320,000 pounds)!

I heard Mr. Fulton telling someone how he had chosen the name. It was named after Robert Livingston's home, which was also called Clermont. This boat was going to change how people traveled. I just knew it! *Revolutionize* is a big word, but there is just no other way to describe what this boat was going to do for the world!

Maybe I'm getting ahead of myself here. How was this boat different from other boats? At this time, boats didn't use engines at all. They were powered by the wind hitting their sails, or sometimes by people rowing them. (Remember our time traveling the Atlantic Ocean with Mr. Fulton? If the wind stopped blowing, it stopped our travel completely.)

This wasn't the case for the *Clermont*! It had an engine to move it forward. Not just any engine, either, but a steam-powered one. I guess I was pretty proud, because I could be the one powering the boat. After all, I can be steam. Huh? What did you say? Well, yes... I can be water. And, yes... I can be ice, too! And snow and sleet and lots of things—including steam!

What is steam you ask? Steam is what happens when water gets really, really hot. We molecules turn to a gaseous state. Maybe you have noticed us when your mom is boiling a pot of water on the stove?

I wondered how the boat was going to run on steam. I mean, we water molecules are pretty tough, but we are also pretty small. Did Robert Fulton think we were going to just get out there and push the boat? I don't think so, mister! The *Clermont* was one big boat. I don't care how many water molecules he would be able to round up, there was no way we were going to be pushing that boat down the river.

I thought maybe he had lost his mind after all. As he stood on the deck of the boat, he went on and on about steam and pistons and paddles. He sounded like a mad scientist as he rushed around the boat's newly installed engine. I couldn't wait to see if he would pull it off. It seemed like a good sign that the boat had not yet sunk to the bottom of the river. I was glad that I was safely in the water, where no harm could befall me.

Hey! Wait a minute! It looked like adventure was going to find me no matter where I went. Mr. Fulton lowered a bucket into the river and filled it with water, managing to scoop me up in the process.

I was now on board the *Clermont*. Why did I have a feeling this was going to be one wild ride?

Now that I was on board the boat, I noticed that there were several other passengers. While Robert seemed like a bundle of energy, his passengers looked much more subdued. In fact, their faces had looks that I couldn't quite put my finger on. Fear? Nervousness? Sadness?

Towards the front of the boat, I noticed Robert Livingston. He had aged a bit in the last few years, but he was still here entertaining guests. He was in his element with all this talking.

"It will be just fine," he said as he comforted one woman who appeared to be quite concerned. "Don't you worry. The *Clermont* is just as safe as any other boat. You have my word." I wondered if Livingston had coerced these poor people into riding the boat, just like he had coerced his French friends into investing in Fulton's work.

She mustered up a faint smile, but I don't think she believed him. I wanted to tell her that I trusted Robert Fulton. I wanted her to know that his experiments always worked. Well... mostly.

Chapter Fourteen

FULL STEAM AHEAD

As Livingston tried to brighten the spirits of the guests, Fulton stayed focused on the task at hand. He shoveled coal into a large contraption, showing the workers how it needed to be done. Once it was full, he struck some flint to light the coals.

Next, he picked up the bucket. Not just any bucket, my bucket. Just what was he planning to do? Before I could spend any more time wondering, he poured the water into a large cylinder attached to the engine.

What was going to happen now? I certainly didn't want to see how the engine worked from the inside, did I? I guess Robert hadn't listened when I told him that under no circumstance was I going to be the one pushing this boat. It was unfair. The other water molecules didn't even seem to know what was going on. I remembered the last time Robert had put me inside something enclosed. It had turned out pretty cool in the end, but it was quite a fright getting there! I hoped this wouldn't be nearly so fast paced.

It wasn't long before things started to get warm. I mean, really warm. Just like my last run-in with Mr. Fulton in his crazy sky rocket. I remembered the coal and the flint, and realized that there must be a raging fire directly below us now. I guess this was how Robert planned to make us into steam before we got around to pushing the boat down the river. His plan was working because pretty soon the molecules towards the top were escaping up the pipe, no longer liquid but now a gas.

Whhhhhoooooaaaa! I felt a little woozy as my body transformed from a liquid to a vapor state. I floated upwards and found myself in a chamber with other steaming water molecules. Pretty soon there were more and more and more.

I don't think Robert had planned for this, because we weren't going to fit in this tiny space. The chamber was getting more and more crowded. This was worse than that crazy cumulonimbus cloud I had found myself in before meeting Ben Franklin!

I was getting so claustrophobic. The walls seemed to be closing in, but it was really just that the space was filling up, faster and faster. There was no hope of escape, and not a single place to move around. I looked over and saw that some of my fellow water molecules were pushing against the wall. "Come on," someone shouted. "Everyone push! This way!"

I did what I was told. Maybe if we all pushed we could break down the wall and escape. The wall! It was moving! I couldn't believe it. Just a tiny bit at

first, but now we really had our momentum going. "Come on everyone! Keep pushing!"

We pushed and pushed and pushed and the wall kept moving. We may not have been pushing the *Clermont*, but we were pushing this wall. Suddenly a space opened up, and we escaped from that little room.

Freedom! We had made it. Fulton couldn't keep us in his water prison for long, could he? As I floated out into the air, I looked around me. Water molecules were congratulating each other and cheering at their victory. Below, I could see the engine working. As I and my fellow steam molecules were pushing, we were moving the pistons of the engine. As the pistons moved, they turned the boat's giant paddle-wheels. I guess steam was moving the boat after all! But not in the way I had thought that we would. It took this clever machine to help us, but we were the ones doing all the work!

I watched as onlookers cheered from the banks. The *Clermont* was steaming along nicely now. I couldn't help but feel a little proud of all my hard work.

I could see the headlines now: "Water Molecule Munford Pushes Steamboat to Fame" or "Munford and Friends Power the *Clermont* on Maiden Journey". I hoped my picture would be in the newspapers. Maybe a nice shot of me on Robert Fulton's shoulder. Or perhaps an action shot of me and the gang pushing the boat. Whatever the case, I knew that after today I was going to be famous!

Later, I was able to watch the boat's journey from my spot in a cloud. Everything went safely, but not quite as I might have expected. For one thing, when people saw the boat coming, they were terrified. I'm not sure why exactly. Maybe it was its huge size. Perhaps it was the trail of black smoke following behind the boiler. Sometimes even the bright orange flames could be seen. I guess it did look a little like a fire-breathing dragon, didn't it?

It seemed that no one had thought to warn the kind country folks about what was coming. As we rounded the bend, I saw a few young boys playing on the shore. At the sight of the *Clermont*, they began to shriek and headed towards the woods.

"Never fear," shouted Fulton from the deck.

“She’s just a boat, boys! A boat!” But it was too late. There was no sign of the boys save the fishing poles they had left in their haste to escape.

The loud noise from the engines must have also been frightening, as more than once we approached people in other boats who seemed frightened by us. Sometimes the passengers on these smaller boats would fall to the deck and put their hands over their heads. Other times, they would abandon their boat completely and swim to shore as if fighting for their lives!

I felt terrible that these people were so

frightened, but on board the attitude was much better. The *Clermont* was steaming along quite nicely, and now that it seemed everyone was going to survive, the atmosphere on deck was starting to perk up.

"By golly, Fulton, you've done it this time!" said one of the passengers.

Fulton just smiled. It was true. He had created a steamboat that was fully functional. It was more efficient than all the steamboats that had gone before him. His hard work had paid off.

My little cloud followed the path of the Hudson River, just as the *Clermont* did. About halfway through the journey, I rained back down onto the boat. The ride was pretty uneventful. The new boat made the 300-mile trip to Albany in just 32 hours. All the passengers looked pretty relieved to get off the boat and back on dry land!

I may not have made it into the papers, but Robert sure did! His name was everywhere, along with pictures of the boat on her maiden voyage. I hated to point out the inaccuracy of the journalism. I mean, didn't those crazy reporters understand who the real heroes were? It wasn't Robert Fulton, inventor and mechanic. Sure, he drew up some fancy sketches and built a neat boat. But did he

get out there and push that thing down the Mighty Hudson? Did he push the pistons? Did he turn the paddlewheels? No, I think not.

The real heroes were the water molecules—the little guys just like me, the ones who did the real work, the manual labor. Those were who the newspapers should have been celebrating!

The next few weeks spent on board the *Clermont* were pretty exciting. The state of New York granted Fulton and Livingston a monopoly. This meant that they were the only steamboat company allowed to travel the Hudson River.

At first, tickets sold pretty slowly. I think everyone was still nervous about the boat. Perhaps the first successful trip had just been a fluke. Maybe the next trip would be the one where the boat ran aground or exploded.

Slowly but surely, however, each journey was a little busier than the next. Pretty soon tickets were selling like hot cakes! Everyone wanted to make the trip to Albany faster than they had ever been able to before.

There was only one tiny little problem with

the *Clermont*... the competition! All the other boats that traveled the Hudson were pretty much out of luck. Who would want to ride those old-fashioned things when they didn't have an engine? No one! Folks did everything in their power to bring the *Clermont* down. Literally! I saw one crazy boat captain ram his vessel into the side of Robert's. It was so small in comparison, it didn't do much damage. Still, the only days that the steamboat spent out of commission were a result of other captains attacking it!

It wasn't long before the state of New York had to make special laws to protect the *Clermont.* They made it a crime to cause any harm to her! This seemed to cut back on the number of attacks. I really had grown to love the *Clermont* while I was board. Not only was she a beautiful boat, but she also hosted some unique passengers. I loved getting to see all the people come and go.

Alas, all good things must come to an end—including my time with Robert Fulton and his steamboat. It was a humid afternoon when I purposely fell into the steam engine. As I escaped

out into the air, I took one last look at the boat. It had been a great adventure, but I couldn't wait to see what would be next!

...and the rest is history.

The *Clermont* may not have been the first steamboat, but it certainly was the best. While Robert Fulton did not actually invent the steamboat, his important improvements made it practical for widespread use. The steamboat was a vital part of the Industrial Revolution, making it easier for the manufacturers sprouting up all over the country to transport their goods and the supplies needed to make them. It also allowed for easier travel of the expanding American continent. While Fulton's inventions did not bring about the world peace that he wanted, he did contribute to ushering in a new era in world development.

As for the *Nautilus*, Robert Fulton was never successful in destroying a ship for Napoleon

Bonaparte. (Although, he did successfully destroy a ship during a test exercise.) After running out of funds for that project, he moved on to the steam engine. Bonaparte, however, was not so lucky. His brilliant military campaigns brought him to power as the leader of France, eventually becoming known as the emperor of that country. However, he met his final defeat at the Battle of Waterloo in 1815 and lived the rest of his live imprisoned by Great Britain.

The Louisiana Purchase was completed in 1803. For the cost of 15 million dollars, Napoleon sold his claim to the entire Louisiana territory, doubling the size of the United States at the time. The Purchase included parts of fourteen states, and was one of the biggest legacies left by President Thomas Jefferson.*

Oh, and in case you were wondering, no one knows exactly why young Robert Fulton bought quicksilver for his experiments!

*To read more about the Louisiana Territory, and its exploration by explorers Lewis and Clark, be sure to check out Munford's adventure, *Munford Meets Lewis & Clark*!

Robert Fulton

Fascinating Facts

- Robert Fulton created several inventions besides the steamboat, including a ropemaker and a dredging machine.

- A ticket to ride the *Clermont* from New York to Albany originally cost seven dollars.

- Napoleon Bonaparte conquered a large portion of the continent of Europe before eventually meeting his defeat. He was sent into exile on the small island of St. Helena.

- Robert Livingston should have signed the Declaration of Independence, but ended up getting called back to New York before he got the chance. He died at the age of sixty-six in 1813, his crowning accomplishments being the Louisiana Purchase and his work with Robert Fulton.

- Robert Fulton married the niece of Robert Livingston, Harriet. They had four children together.

- Fulton and Livingston expanded their steamboat business to include several other rivers and the Chesapeake Bay.

- One of Fulton's last projects before his death was a battleship for the United States military.

- Fulton died from pneumonia in 1815, after pulling a friend from icy water.

Author's Note

Sharing the Vision of Munford

I met Josh and Cindy Wiggers, the fine folks behind Geography Matters, while I was still in high school. Their kids and I went to church together and were becoming fast friends. It wasn't long before I went to the Wiggers house for a visit. Josh made quite an impression on me. First, he insisted that everyone call him Uncle Josh. Second, every conversation, it seemed, ended up turning into a geography drill. "What is the smallest country in the world? What is the capital of Zambia? What country is located between France and Spain?" Needless to say, all of these questions were a little overwhelming, but I kept going back for more visits and more geography drills.

Uncle Josh began telling me about a vision he had of a character he named Munford. He had first dreamed up the little water molecule many years before in a moment of inspiration while driving on the highway in the rain. Because Munford was water, he could be anywhere at anytime in history. By following his adventures, kids could learn about science, history, and geography. There would be almost no limit to what Munford could do. The only problem was that Uncle Josh hadn't been able to find a writer that was a good match for Munford. He had heard that writing was a hobby of mine, and wanted me to give it a try. I'm not sure exactly why he chose to take a chance on me. I was only a sophomore in high school! He must have liked my sample chapter, though, because he asked me to finish the book (*Munford Meets Lewis and Clark*) and then write others (*The Klondike Gold Rush, The American Revolution*, and more to come...).

It was 2002 when I first set pen to page and wrote Munford's first adventure. Since then, Uncle Josh and the rest of the Wiggers family became like a part of my extended family. Geography Matters has grown and flourished as one of the best homeschooling publishers on the market today. Munford himself has gone through many changes, thanks to multiple revisions, illlustrators, and improvements.

Munford, who is actually a water molecule, is often referred to and portrayed as a water drop. A water drop is actually made of many water molecules, so I took some artistic license by calling him a drop. It is easier to understand and visualize Munford as a drop rather than a teeny, tiny, molecule that cannot be seen with the naked eye.

My hope for Munford is that he will teach your children without them even realizing how much they are learning. Who knows, if they ever have the chance to meet Uncle Josh, or someone like him, perhaps they will be able to answer those pesky geography, history, or science questions with pride.

Munford's Other Adventures

The American Revolution

In this adventure, Munford travels to colonial America and experiences first hand the events leading to the American Revolution. He meets famed American Founding Fathers, such as Samuel Adams, Thomas Jefferson, and George Washington. He joins the Sons of Liberty under cover of night to dump tea into Boston Harbor. He tags along for Paul Revere's most famous ride, and even becomes a part of the Declaration of Independence in a way that you might not expect!

The Klondike Gold Rush

In this adventure, Munford finds himself slap into the middle of the Klondike Gold Rush. He catches gold fever on this dangerous, yet thrilling, adventure. Meet some of the Gold Rush's most famous characters, like gold baron Alex McDonald or the tricky villain named Soapy Smith. Take a ride on the Whitehorse Rapids, and help Munford as he pans for gold. This is an adventure you won't soon forget!

More and More to Come . . .

Look for more adventures in this exciting series as Munford's journey through time and territory continues around the world.

Other Books by Jamie Aramini

Eat Your Way Around the World
by Jamie Aramini

Get out the sombrero for your Mexican fiesta! Chinese egg rolls… corn pancakes from Venezuela… fried plantains from Nigeria. All this, and more, is yours when you take your family on a whirlwind tour of over thirty countries in this unique international cookbook. Includes a full meal of recipes from each country. Recipes are easy to follow, and ingredients are readily available. Jam-packed with delicious dinners, divine drinks, and delectable desserts, this book is sure to please.

Geography Through Art
by Sharon Jeffus and Jamie Aramini

This is the ultimate book of U.S. and international art projects. Join your children on an artistic journey to more than twenty-five countries spanning six continents (includes over a dozen United States projects). *Geography Through Art* would make a lasting addition to your home or school library. Use this book as an exciting way to supplement any study of geography, history, or social studies. You'll find yourself reaching for this indispensable guide again and again to delight and engage students in learning about geography through the culture and art of peoples around the world.

About the Author

Jamie Aramini is the author of *Eat Your Way Around the World*, *Geography Through Art* with Sharon Jeffus, and the *Adventures of Munford* series. She graduated co-valedictorian of her high school class and was a Kentucky Governor's Scholar. She is currently raising her two sons, a flock of chickens, and a miniature Schnauzer named Sophie. Her hobbies include organic gardening, cooking, and teaching writing at her local homeschool co-op. Visit www.jamiearamini.com to learn more about Jamie.

About the Illustrator

Emily Lefferts is a homeschool graduate from Sutton, Massachusetts. She is currently studying visual arts with a concentration in illustration at Gordon College. Her courses at Gordon have taken her to Italy where she spent a semester studying art. After graduation, she hopes to continue working as an illustrator. She lives at home with seven siblings, four dogs, and two very patient parents.